# QUEST FOR CLOUD KINGDOM

## A Petey Potette Training Tale

**Author**
**Brice Sanderford**

**Illustrator**
**Mark Rosenbohm**

Hi, my name is Drew and this is my friend Sue.
And, boy do we have a story for you!

I was still in diapers and trying to potty train.
But I was finding the training boring and plain.

I liked my diapers, what's the big deal?
Except when they're wet, I don't like how they feel.

One day the Cloud King came
and took Sue away.
He said "Until you learn to potty
like a big boy, with me Sue will stay."

Don't worry Sue,
I'm coming for you.
I'll rescue you from Cloud Kingdom
if it's the last thing I do.

WATER KINGDOM

TREE
KINGDOM

MOUNTAIN KINGDOM

CLOUD
KINGDOM

N

E

S

But where is Cloud Kingdom?
It seems far away.
I wish I had someone to show me the way.

Then I remembered
mommy had a magical frien
Who had plenty of kindness
and wisdom to lend.

With a poof he appeared,
and he bowed very sweetly.
It was the great wizard Potette,
but he said call him Petey.

So with a whiz and a snap to Cloud Kingdom we went.
We'd rescue Sue, with time on my training well spent.

We arrived at Cloud Kingdom and couldn't get in.
It seemed to me like there was no way to win.

Petey told me with time we would break down the gate.
Like the potty, the key to magic is to be patient and wait

With a snap and a crash the gates fell apart.
It seemed like patience was a good place to start.

The castle was far away,
 so we hopped on a wagon.
It was all going great,
 till we were met by a dragon.

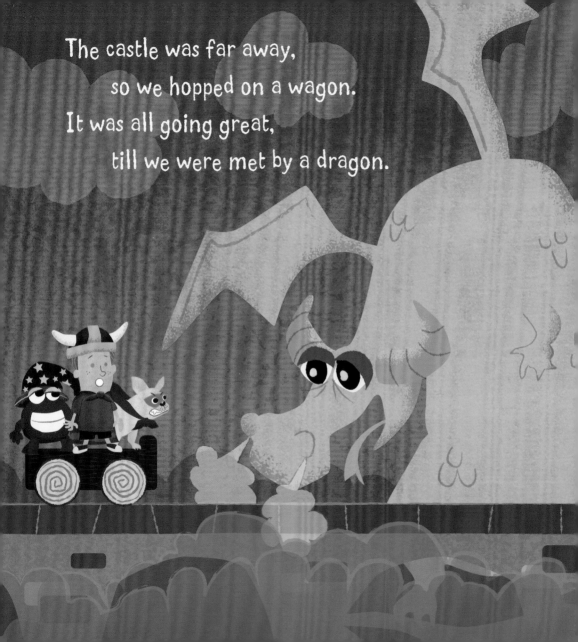

Like a nasty potty, the dragon was huge, stinky and scary.
But I had a powerful item Petey said I should carry.

It was the magical Potette and its ways Petey would teach
Once I learned to use it, potty training would be within rea

So I used the Potette
as my mighty shield
I beat the great dragon
with the new power I wield.

Finally to the Cloud King's castle we arrived.
I was scared, but knew that Sue was inside.

Don't worry Drew, just use all that you've learned.
Remember that victory is not given, but earned.

I said to the Cloud King "Give my friend to me.
With the Power of Potette, I'll beat you, you'll see."

With a bang and a crackle, I used my magical might.
It gave the Cloud King a mighty, mighty big fright.

"Drew it is you!" I heard Sue say.
"I've come to get you, and we're leaving today."

The next day I woke up, after the craziest dream.
I had learned a great lesson, but what did it mean?

Then I remembered it all,
with pride and joy.
Petey and Sue had taught me
to be a big boy!